Order this book online at www.trafford.com
or email orders@trafford.com

Most Trafford titles are also available at major online book retailers.

Printed in Victoria, BC, Canada.

ISBN: 978-1-4251-7646-4

*Our mission is to efficiently provide the world's finest, most comprehensive book publishing
service, enabling every author to experience success. To find out how to publish your book, your
way, and have it available worldwide, visit us online at www.trafford.com*

Trafford rev. 7/22/2010

Trafford
PUBLISHING® www.trafford.com

North America & international
toll-free: 1 888 232 4444 (USA & Canada)
phone: 250 383 6864 ♦ fax: 812 355 4082

Lena Jacobs - Kwitelut-t

nee Band

1910 - 2008

Texwlam na ta7am ti sxwexwiyam t7alhi: Chesha7, Si7l, Sata7, Siyay. An wanaxwstas i7xw ta smenhems lha menilh. Na wa chenchenstas i7xw ta skwekwiyintsutswit tima tkwi nexw7usayelh ta s7ulh snichim wa usuntas ta menmen-chet.

This story really happened in her lifetime, dear Mom, Gran, Auntie, Friend. She had great pride in and respect for all her friends and relatives. She supported each and every one in what they were doing and she took it upon herself to help in teaching our language to all of our young ones.

Storyteller: Kwitelut t ~ Lena Jacobs
Original illustrations by: Xwalacktun ~ Rick Harry

Elders Advisory:
Ta na wa Xwniwn ta a Imats ~ Teachings for Your Grandchildren, Elders Advisory
Nekwsaliya ~ Mrs. Margaret Locke, Tiyaltalut ~ Mrs. Audrey Rivers, Chiyalhiya ~
Mrs. Lila Johnston, Kwinakatemaat ~ Mrs. Lucille Nicholson, Nekwnakwelut ~ Barbara
Charlie, Tseltselmat ~ Addie Kermeen, Xatsalano Tanayno ~ Alec Williams,
Skwetsatenat ~ Valerie Moody

Edited with:
T'naxwtn ~ Peter Jacob/Linguist, Kirsten Baker-Williams/School Administrator,
Vanessa Campbell/Squamish Language Program.

Produced by:
Skwxwu7mesh uxwumixw Ns7eyxnitm ta Snewiyalh ~ Squamish Nation Education Dept.,
under the direction of Siyámiya iy Snitelwet ~ Deborah Jacobs.

Formatting and Media Production by:
Norman Guerrero Jr., Xwáchtenaat ~ Kathy Joseph-LaRock and Kwítelut ~ Lorraine Louis
Marianne Bullied, Strang Burton, and Madeline Hannan-Leith.

Yú7yus Slúlum - KillerWhale Song by Latáshkinm ~ Maurice Nahanee, used with permission.

*Collage image for Lena's Dedication page by Juniper Groves, Skwxwu7mesh uxwumixw ~
Squamish Nation Communications, used with permission.*

*Back Cover Image shows Eslha7án/Mission IR#1: Racing canoe, beach at North Vancouver BC
circa 1950. Squamish Nation archives, used with permission.*

Chen x̱wéx̱wiy̓am̓ ta asxw. Ses a kwélashtm
tkwi n sísi7t T'enáx̱wtn, kwélashtas kwélhi,
kwélhi asxw na7 tkwa áyalhḵw.

Ses men k̲w'uy ...álhi asxw.   Ses men nam ch'it ta, tan sísi7 kw'áchtas.   Na wa es7á7tsiw̓an!   Na melh menkw tsixw kwis xweys ...lhi ásxw-ul-lh.

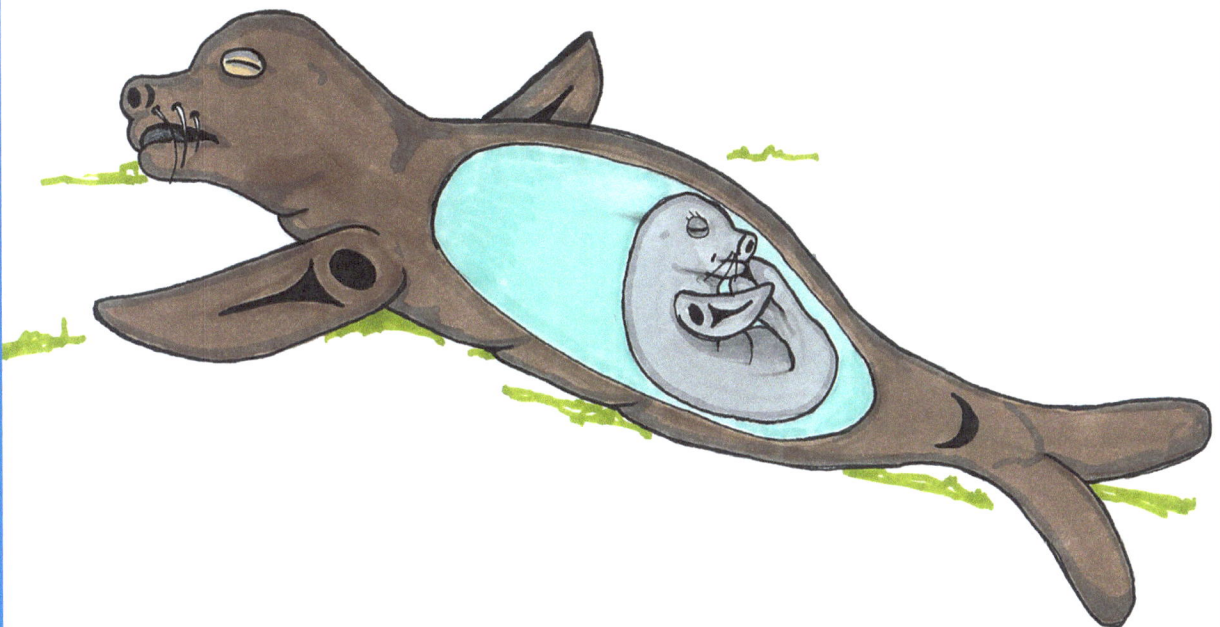

The seal died. When my uncle went to take a closer look
he saw that it was carrying a baby.
So right away he went to deliver that baby seal.

Chet yi<u>k</u>w i7<u>x</u>w na7 wa ínexw. Ses men p'í7tas tsi tsi lhách'tens.

We all went closer to see... he got out his knife...

Ses men kw'ích'intas álhi asxw, t'áxwaṅtas ta ásxw-ul-lh! I7xw ta stá7uxwlh, chet wa kw'awcht. Ses mi uts'k tiná7 t7álhi chésha7s, álhi ásxw-ul-lh ses men mi xwey álhi ásxw-ul-lh.

... he made a cut... and out came the baby seal!
All of us kids got to see! Out she came from her mom!
Just like that! The seal pup was born! A little girl seal!

Menkw iẏím, hiyí... álhi ásxw-ul-lh! Na siẇáẏ wa t'íchim álhi ásxw-ul-lh! Men i7x̱w, men i7x̱w ta stá7uxwlh na wa naṁ cheycháẏstas! Naṁ shú7shukw'um sḵ'u7 tl'a nímalh! Yiḵw naṁ shú7shukw'um, na chayntúmulhas álhi ásxw-ul-lh.

But oh! She was so strong! And big! That little girl seal! She was swimming right away! And she would follow the children! All of the kids! She would swim with us! If you went swimming... there she'd be following us around!

l7xw chet na wa tl'i7s lhi ásxw-ul-lh! Chet nam̓ iw̓ás kwi sts'ukwi7úl-lh kwis ílhens chet álhi ásxw-ul-lh.

Oh! We all loved that baby seal so much!
We went fishing for it to get little fish to feed it!

Ha (u) chet naṁ shú7shukw'um, i yi<u>k</u>w nekw na7 álhi ásxw-ul-lh cheycháẏstúmulhas. Na wa ṁi kwi staẏch-chet. Na wa ṁi iẏáẏach i tkwi staẏch-chet.

And so it went...
if you went swimming there she was following us around!
She'd get on our backs and she'd hold on!

Na ṁi tkwétsi S<u>x</u>elhnát. Na ṁi kwen sísi7
tsuntúmulhas i7<u>x</u>w ta stá7uxwlh, "Naṁ chap
kw'enmáylh. I7<u>x</u>w chap naṁ kw'enmáylh!" Ses
chet men i7<u>x</u>w naṁ uys ta kw'enmáylháẃtxw.

One Sunday my uncle came and told all of us children,
'Go and pray! All of you go and pray!'
And so we all went off to church.

Nilh yi<u>k</u>w wa cheycháy̓a<u>k</u>em lhi Sealiya! Na men nam̓ kat, cheycháy̓a<u>k</u>em nam̓ uys ta kw'enmáylháw̓txw! Yi<u>k</u>w wá7u wa kwáchem, cheycháy̓a<u>k</u>em tl'a nímelh! Stl'i7s kwis nam̓s uys ta kw'enmáylháw̓txw.

And there she was!... Sealiya was following us! She climbed the steps, following along after us to the Church! And all the time she was hollering, bellowing as she followed us! She really wanted to come along into the Church.

Ses men tsut kwin sisi7t: "Aaa ...haw ḵw'ap ṁi uys! Haw ḵw'ap ṁi uys!" Kw'ay kwis ḵ'al's álhi asxw! Ses men ṁi uts'ḵstem tkwi n sisi7t! Men a:n kwáchem! An chet wa tl'i7s ti ásxw-ul-lh!

But Uncle yelled out, "Don't Bring Her In!!! Don't Bring Her In!!!"
But she wouldn't obey! So Uncle had to put her outside!
She hollered and hollered! Oh... We loved that baby seal so much!

Ses men ṁi shewaẏ álhi ásxw-ul-lh.

And the baby seal grew!

Na huy ásxw-ul-lh. Na asxw.

Soon she wasn't a baby seal anymore!
She was a Seal!

Na tsixw kwétsi nch'u7 syeȽánem, nekw nta7áẃn álhi Sealiya kwis naṁs ḵẃú7ntsut ta síiyaẏs, ta es7ásxw.

After a year it occurred to Sealiya to go and join her friends the seals.

Chet i7x̱w nam̓ kw'awcht kwi seskw huyá7. I
aa kwi sḵwálwen-chet kw-huyá7 lhi ha7lh
siyáy̓-chet, wa sḵ'u7 tl'a nímalh tl'et
ḵw'eshétsut. Na huy tsin sx̱wéx̱wiy̓ám̓.

And so all of us watched as she went off...
but oh we were so sad hearted as we saw our playmate leave.
So... this is... THE END... of my story.

www.ingramcontent.com/pod-product-compliance
Lightning Source LLC
Chambersburg PA
CBHW040230070426
42448CB00033B/265